# Spot the Difference

# Tails

## Diyan Leake

**www.heinemann.co.uk/library**
Visit our website to find out more information about Heinemann Library books.

To order:
☎ Phone 44 (0) 1865 888066
Send a fax to 44 (0) 1865 314091
 Visit the Heinemann Bookshop at www.heinemann.co.uk/library to browse our
 catalogue and order online.

First published in Great Britain by Heinemann Library,
Halley Court, Jordan Hill, Oxford OX2 8EJ, part of Harcourt
Education. Heinemann is a registered trademark of Harcourt
Education Ltd.

Editorial: Diyan Leake and Cassie Mayer
Design: Joanna Hinton-Malivoire
Picture research: Erica Martin
Production: Duncan Gilbert

Originated by Chroma Graphics (Overseas) Pte Ltd
Printed and bound in China by South China Printing Co. Ltd

ISBN 978 0 4311 9138 6

11 10 09 08 07
10 9 8 7 6 5 4 3 2 1

**British Library Cataloguing in Publication Data**
Leake, Diyan
Tails. - (Spot the difference)
1. Tail - Juvenile literature 2. Animals - Juvenile
literature
I. Title
591.4

**Acknowledgements**
The publishers would like to thank the following for permission
to reproduce photographs: FLPA Norbert Wu/Minden
Pictures p. **5**; Getty Images/The Image Bank/Frans
Lemmens p. **15**; Getty Images/Photographers Choice
p. **17**; Jupiter Images/Premium Stock pp. **9**, **23** bottom;
Nature Picture Library pp. **4** (David Pike), **6** (Michael Pitts),
**8** (Anup Shah), **10** (Terry Andrewartha), **14** (Luiz Claudio
Marigo), **16** (Michael W. Richards), **22** (Terry Andrewartha),
**23**mid (Terry Andrewartha); Nature Picture Library/
Premaphotos p. **19**; Nature Picture Library/Reinhard/
ARCO p. **11**; NHPA/Nigel J. Dennis p **12**; Photolibrary/
Animals Animals/Earth Scenes pp. **18**, **23** bottom;
Photolibrary/Picture Press p. **13**; Photolibrary/Konrad
Wothe pp. **7**, **22**, **23** top; Punchstock p. **20**; Punchstock/
Stock Connection p. **21**.

Cover photograph of a cheetah reproduced with permission
of Nature Picture Library/ Anup Shah.

Every effort has been made to contact copyright holders
of any material reproduced in this book. Any omissions will
be rectified in subsequent printings if notice is given to the
publishers.

# Contents

# What is a tail?

A tail is part of a body.
Some animals have tails.

Tails are usually at the end of the animal's body.

# Why do animals have a tail?

Animals use their tail to move.

Animals use their tail to balance.

# Different tails

Tails come in many shapes and sizes.

This is a pig.

It has a curly tail.

This is a squirrel.
It has a bushy tail.

This is a rat.

It has a smooth tail.

Can you spot the difference?

This is a lemur.

It has a stripy tail.

This is a leopard.

It has a spotty tail.

# Amazing tails

spider monkey

This is a monkey.

It can hold on with its tail.

This is a scorpion.

It can sting with its tail.

Can you spot the difference?

rattle

This is a snake.

It makes a noise with its tail.

16

This is a peacock.

It shows off with its tail.

This is a deer.
It warns other deer of danger with
its tail.

This is a lizard.
Its tail can fall off.

# Do people have a tail?

People do not have a tail.

They use their legs and feet to move.

People have arms and hands.
People use their arms to balance.

# Can you remember?

Which animal has a bushy tail?

Which animal uses its tail to balance?

# Picture glossary

 **balance** keep steady and not fall

 **bushy** covered with thick, fluffy hair

 **curly** with a twist

 **warn** tell others that something is dangerous before it happens

# Index

**Notes for parents and teachers**

**Before reading**

Talk to the children about animals with tails. Why do they think animals have tails? What does it mean if a dog wags its tail?

**After reading**

- Sing the song: Rabbit ain't got no tail at all, tail at all, tail at all. Rabbit ain't got no tail at all – just a powder puff!
- Draw an outline of a donkey on a large piece of paper. Make a tail by plaiting some wool. Put some Blu-tack on one end of the tail. Blindfold a child and turn the child round once. Give the child the tail and challenge them to stick it on the donkey. Then remove the blindfold and let them see the results.
- Cut out some pictures of animals with tails. Don't show the children the pictures but ask them a riddle – for example, I have a strong thick tail which helps me swim. I have a big mouth and lots of sharp teeth. I live in rivers in Africa. What am I?